The Next Step

REAL LIFE STORIES OF OVERCOMING FINANCIAL HEARTACHE

By Dr. Bill Clark

WITH THE ASSISTANCE OF MOM, SALLIE CLARK

Cover design & book layout by Splash of Design

www.splashofdesign.net

Drawings used by permission of CopyDoodles.com

FORWARD

During my thirty years of pastoral ministry I have seen the heartache and grief experienced by individuals who lose their spouse. Equally disorienting are the effects of divorce on individuals as they recoil from the emotional, physical, and financial impact that has changed their world. At Gateway, and at many other churches, we have developed a team of volunteers who provide sensitive care during this difficult time. We seek to put many tools at their disposal as they help those grieving their loss recover and walk forward into a new reality working to restore happiness and health in their shattered world.

The experience and expertise of Bill Clark is expressed through his practical wisdom and advice presented in this book. I believe it will be another tool to help people heal and recover from their grief, a tool that has been long overdue.

My dad passed away at 62 leaving my mom a very young widow. She had a great network of support to walk with her as she processed her new reality but a practical tool to speak to _The Next Steps_ she would have to address was missing. While she had good advisors it would have been so helpful to have a resource like this book to help her be aware of the issues needing to be addressed as she faced a new and unexpected future. At a time of such deep grief a resource of help for her, me, and others as we were advising her would have been a valuable resource to help point her in the right direction for solutions to the difficult issues she was immediately facing.

Across the broad spectrum of issues on the plate of life, issues that impact our employment, family, and finances, one thing can support and help them all. . . preparation. This book will not only serve as a tool to help those walking through the loss and grief of death or divorce but it will serve as a tool to help families prepare for the reality of issues they will face and be prepared for the future.

On behalf of all those who will benefit from your open sharing and expertise, thank you Bill. For those needing the resource of this book my heart goes out to you in this time of loss and my prayerful hope is for your comfort and peace as you address the difficult decisions you face with the help of loved ones and friends.

— Tom Lane
Executive Senior Pastor, Gateway Church, Southlake, Texas

The Next Step has been prepared using real life scenarios coupled with sound professional advice. Dr. Clark has addressed in detail the many items and situations we all will eventually face in one form or another. Additionally, he has provided the reader with well thought- out suggestions for both planning ahead and dealing with issues that will arise if no plan has been previously discussed. His knowledge, expertise and experiences have provided an excellent opportunity for Bill to compile, in one publication, a virtual 'how to' manual for those who get lost in the sea of details that must be dealt with when we face life's changes and challenges. This book is a 'must read' for everyone.

— Rick Allen
Allen Family Funeral Options, Plano, Texas

We all think our finances and affairs are in order until an accident, health reversal, or death occurs. Then we wish we or our parents had paid more attention to details. The Next Step is a complete financial guide that takes you through the steps you need to take. It is an indispensable tool for everyone.

— Kerby Anderson, National Director
Probe Ministries International

Losing a loved one, especially a spouse, is the most devastating thing that can happen to an individual. If a couple has not made adequate preparation for this event, which can come at any age, the loss can be overwhelming. As a Funeral Practitioner for almost fifty years, I can attest that being prepared, with the proper legal documents and final arrangements planning, will make this loss much more bearable. The material in this book should be required reading for everyone regardless of age, marital status or financial position.

— Ben Coleman
Funeral Director, Grove Hill Funeral Home & Memorial Park

Table of Contents

Various documents-spreadsheets mentioned in this book are available on the web site.
Visit www.drbillclark.com and click on *The Next Step tab*.

ACKNOWLEDGEMENTS

Even though I am a financial advisor with thirty years experience, this book would not have been possible without a special group of people. I want to give thanks to my mother Sallie Clark, herself recently widowed and also to the Texas ladies from my Tyler and Frisco focus groups. They took the time to speak honestly and openly about their experiences. Some subject matter proved very hard for them to discuss, as it was still fresh and therefore painful, but they never held back as they shared their comments and stories with only the hope of helping others in similar circumstances.

Thanks again, ladies! This book is for all of you.

Dr. Bill Clark

INTRODUCTION

First, let me tell you a little about myself and my reasons for writing this book. I am Dr. Bill Clark, Founder and CEO of Clark Financial Group, Inc. in Frisco, Texas. I have been in the estate planning and financial services industry for thirty years, and it has been my mission to serve and educate pre-retirees and retirees on their financial needs.

From the American College, I earned the Chartered Life Underwriter and the Chartered Financial Consultant designations. I hold a master's degree in education and a doctorate in psychology.

I specialize in financial and estate planning, helping clients avoid paying unnecessary taxes - such as income, Social Security, and estate taxes. Avoiding probate and increasing spendable income is another important part of my practice. Finally, I help seniors avoid Medicaid "spend-down" of their hard earned assets for nursing home care.

I also conduct hundreds of workshops that provide a platform whereby seniors can learn how to protect their assets, increase their income, avoid paying unnecessary taxes, and provide guarantees to their assets. I strive to constantly keep my clients updated on the latest tax strategies and changes in Washington, including money-saving techniques that affect them.

The need for this type of book was brought to my attention with the passing of my father. My mother suddenly found herself alone and responsible for many of the details my father took care of for her. I, of course, stepped in and made sure she was on track financially. Still, the experience got me thinking about other spouses who might not be so well informed or who might not have someone who could walk them through such difficult things with insight and wisdom. So I asked my mother to co-author this book with me.

We conducted several focus groups with widows and widowers, discussing the difficult questions they all seemed to have when they faced the hardship of losing their spouse. We wanted to know what information they desperately needed and what caused them the most worry. Knowing this and hearing their stories helped considerably in writing this book.

In addition, I realized that many singles - by choice or circumstance - might also benefit from this important information. This could help them get things in order after a divorce or assist their children or loved ones who would be left with the task of dealing with their estates. These things are not pleasant to dwell on, but they are essential for one to be aware of. Take the time to carefully consider the advice in the following pages; it can spare you and your loved ones much heartache in the future.

Important First Steps

Mary & Jim's Story

It is funny what the body can do when it's forced to. The body reacting in miraculous ways is something I have read about in stories, but after experiencing it myself, I believe the stories a little more earnestly.

It happened when a person I barely knew informed me that my husband of fifteen years was very sick. This stranger in a bright white coat explained that the man I had loved for over twenty-two years had prostate cancer and now had only a short time to live. All I could do was stare off into space. I kept thinking I should be devastated; I kept wondering where my tears were. I suppose the best explanation of my reaction would be that my head told my heart that heartbreak and tears would have to wait.

From the moment I heard the diagnosis, I knew what I had to do. My role in our marriage changed instantly, and I needed to become a rock. Jim had been the stable one, but now he needed a pillar to support him. No matter what, heartache and confusion were not going to interfere - not when he needed me the most.

The first thing we did was have a heart-to-heart talk. Together, Jim and I discussed my plan of action. First, I needed a Power of Attorney which is a legal authorization that would allow me to make legal decisions and act in Jim's best interest. He had always handled our finances and investments;

I didn't know anything except that we had had a lawyer draw up wills several years ago. I knew where Jim kept the lawyer's contact information, so I called and made an appointment with him.

He informed me that I needed to bring a detailed list of our assets and liabilities to the appointment. Jim and I made a list, and he told me most of the information I would need was on his home computer. All the instructions and passwords for the computer were listed in his ledger in his office. One evening after saying good night to Jim in the hospital, I sat at his desk in our home and pulled out the ledger. There I found all of our accounts listed, website addresses, passwords, ID's, the name of our accountant, credit cards and the balances and how those are paid each month. I could not believe how much information was there and how many things Jim regularly took care of for me. I felt so stupid that it took his becoming ill for me to even show interest in our finances. Why didn't I ask about these matters long ago?

Asking "why" was not being productive, so I forced myself to move on and turned on the printer/copier and copied several pages from the ledger to take to the lawyer's office. I then flipped on the computer and watched it come to life. After typing in Jim's ID and password, I followed his detailed instructions and pulled up our bank account. Once I was successfully logged in, I viewed our checking and savings accounts, reviewed a list of the bills Jim paid online, and checked a couple of our credit card accounts that we have with the bank. I made notes on all the information I thought that the lawyer would need and logged out of the bank website.

Next, I opened my email and wrote to our accountant explaining Jim's medical condition and asked for his assistance in getting necessary paperwork/documents together. I also explained my time limitation, since I had to have these things before my appointment with the lawyer.

It was by far the hardest thing I ever had to do, making these lists while not allowing my emotions to surface. But I had to remain focused.

Richard & Georgia's Story

I was the only breadwinner since Georgia and I were married some forty-five years ago. Shortly after we were married, Georgia took it upon herself to deposit my paycheck into our joint account, pay all the bills, balance our checkbook, purchase anything we needed for the home from groceries to furniture, and basically oversee all of our financial matters. She would seek my input on major purchases, which bills to pay first, or why various credit cards charged certain interest rates, but for the most part, Georgia took care of everything.

This system worked well for us, but when she died suddenly after battling complications from a severe case of pneumonia, my life was changed forever in more ways than one. I was totally devastated and now completely alone. Even as I was trying to grasp the reality that she was really gone, I was being handed stacks of medical bills and hospital bills for me to pay or review. It dawned on me that I did not have the foggiest idea where I stood financially. I didn't even know where the checkbook was located, much less what we owed or how much was in our savings account.

I was embarrassed to even admit to the bank manager that I didn't know our account information. It became apparent to the banker that I desperately needed his assistance. Luckily, my signature was on the account, so getting the needed information turned out to be easier than I first thought.

However, the hard part came when I was trying to find the answers to other important financial questions, beginning with where the mortgage information, insurance policies, car titles/paperwork, and more were located. Finding them and dealing with all the details on each was something I did not enjoy doing. But one by one, I contacted each credit card, savings plan, insurance policyholder, utility companies and mortgage company. I asked questions about each one, taking notes and changing the names on each of these accounts. These calls took me weeks to wade through and many hours of phone conversations with individuals who were not always polite or helpful. I felt like I was drop kicked into a financial whirlwind. I was forced to deal with these unpleasant things on top of making the funeral arrangements and dealing with the reality of losing my wife. In hindsight, I wish I had been more aware of our financial standing.

From Dr. Bill

If I were to ask you right now what insurance company your car is covered with, would you know? If you don't, would you know where to find the information? What about the account number or the agent's name and phone number?

You can probably see where I'm going with this, and you would be surprised by how many people don't know much about their personal and very important information. In the example stories above, you see how quickly lives can change and how much harder it is to deal with an emergency situation if you have to begin "financial forensic maneuvers" to get all the information and documents you need together. So begin now by asking questions and getting answers.

Don't know where to begin? You are not alone. I have listed some questions here to get you started. You will likely think of more, so write them down. Don't get so overwhelmed that you put it off for *another time*. Don't rush, but don't put it off any longer.

Sample Questions:

1. Where are our policies for home and car insurance, plus the account numbers and contact information for the agent and policy company?

2. What about all information on health policies?

3. Where are our bank accounts? What are the account numbers?

4. What bills do we pay each month? I need the list and the account numbers, plus balances due and payment due dates, etc.

5. Do we pay bills online? If so, what bank? What is the website, logon and password information?

6. How do I pay online?

7. If manual checks, where are they and how do I fill them out?

8. Where is all of our various credit card information? (i.e., account numbers, websites, login, contact numbers, balances, etc.)

9. Where is all of our important tax information? For example who does our taxes? And how do I contact them? Where are all the past copies?

10. What is our monthly income?

11. Where is the deed to the house?

12. What is the password and logon information for the computer?

13. What websites do we use for accounts and investments?

14. What are the user names and passwords for all websites we use?

15. What monthly services do we have? (i.e.; lawn care, home security system, handyman, plumber, etc.) I need all contact information for these.

16. Do we have a financial planner or advisor? What exactly do they do for us? How would I contact him/her for assistance if I needed it? What do I expect from him/her?

17. Do we have a trust? What is it exactly?

18. What about Power of Attorney?

19. Do we have life insurance benefits?

20. What about a nursing home policy?

21. What about our funeral arrangements/plans and what about funeral policies?

The process of gathering all the important documents in your life can be overwhelming. The best thing to do is take it one step at a time. The following chart can help you gather the right documents and important information you will need. This example chart can be simply written in a notebook and stored in your home office, or for your convenience, we have included a link on our website where you can download this spreadsheet along with several other helpful spreadsheets.

Visit **WWW.DRBILLCLARK.COM** and click on *The Next Step tab*.

After saving the file to your home computer, simply enter your information and save the document in a location that is easy to remember and access. However you choose to store this information is fine. But recording all this in one central location will help you immensely when the time comes.

If you do not have internet access, you can also contact our office and we will send you a package of printed spreadsheets that you can fill out and keep in your files.

> **Also remember to let your beneficiaries know of this record of information so they will have it in case you yourself become ill or incapacitated.**

DOCUMENT/ITEM	FIRM NAME	ACCOUNT NO.	AGENT/CONTACT NAME	AGENT/CONTACT NUMBER	WEBSITE	LOGIN	PASSWORD
Life Insurance	United Heathcare						
House Insurance	Allstate						
Care Insurance	Allstate						
Health Insurance	United Healthcare						
IRA	Vanguard						
Stock 1	Company X						
Stock 2	Company X						
Stock 3	Company X						
Investment Property	Sierra						
House Deed	Citibank						
Electric	CoServ						
Water	Town of...						
Gas	Town of...						
Cable	Moore's Cable						
Phone	ATT						
Internet	ATT						
Doctor	Dr. Patterson						
Hospital	Baylor Medical						
Funeral Planning							
Home Security Company							
Lawn Care	All Done Yard Care						
Sprinkler System	Xtream						
Taxes	Turbo Tax						
Car Title	Chase						
Bank	Chase						
Savings	Chase						
Securities	Savor						
Business Advisor	John Doe						

15

"TOO SUBTLE?"

What Do I Do First?

Mike & Jean's Story

The day Mike passed away was a typical June day. I was working around the house while Mike, settled in his favorite chair, was watching the NBA Championships. Out of the corner of my eye, I suddenly saw Mike slump down into his chair. I called out his name as I ran over to him, but he didn't respond. Grabbing the phone, I quickly dialed 911. Once they arrived, the paramedics were able to revive Mike momentarily and transport him to the hospital, but despite their best efforts to save him, Mike did not make it.

I arrived just moments behind the ambulance. As I ran in, a nurse pulled me aside and informed me that Mike was in fact gone. I was caught so off guard. I remember the pain being so bad I thought my heart would explode. Suddenly my wonderful life came to a total standstill, and I felt completely paralyzed. I was unable to even comprehend how to function or survive without Mike. I felt like the air was suddenly sucked out of the room. What would I do now?

I had never experienced any real tragedy in my life prior to this, so I had no clue what I needed to do as I sat dazed in my car in the hospital parking lot. I did manage to make it home, and after a few phone calls to family, it dawned on me to contact our financial advisor. I knew he could advise me on what to do now.

Thankfully, he was in the office when I called and was able to talk with me. As he patiently walked me through some of what I needed to do, I jotted down some quick notes. I was an emotional and mental wreck. If it had not been for his wise counsel and advice, who knows the kind of mess I could have ended up in? It was not easy to deal with all the details while grieving but I, unfortunately, did not have a choice. There were so many things that I "thought" I knew, but I just didn't know. I was really scattered for a couple of years, but thanks to his help I came through it okay.

From Dr. Bill

Are you in the same position as Jean? If so, here are some important things to do shortly after the loss of your loved one.

1. First

Below is a short list of important documents. A more complete list is given in the appendix beginning on page 91. Locate each document and place into one central file/location for easy access.

(If you are doing this pre-death, gather these documents and keep in a lock box, fire proof cabinet or safety deposit box. If you need keys to access them, label them clearly and put on a key ring.)

- Life Insurance Policies
- Wills
- Birth Certificates
- Death Certificate (when available)
- Social Security Card
- Retirement Plan Documentation
- Real Estate Deeds
- Car Insurance Policies
- Homeowner's Insurance Policy
- Divorce Agreements
- Power of Attorney
- Trust Documents

- Loan Documents
- Mortgage Documents
- Tax Returns
- Safety Deposit Box key & information
- Bank Statements
- Brokerage Statements
- Stock Certificates
- Current Billing Statements
- Leasing Documents
- Partnership Agreements
- Marriage Certificates
- Funeral Burial Plans

2. Second

Below is a list of agencies or individuals you will need to contact informing them that there has been a death.

❶ FINANCIAL ADVISOR:

A true financial advisor will coordinate your investments, budgeting, legal documents, accounting, and insurance, including life, home and auto. It is best to have a point person or firm that will have your best interest at heart. When you contact your advisor, tell him of your loss. He should have most of your contacts phone numbers (legal, accounting, and insurance), in his files. He will coordinate with you and your other advisors to have accounts changed into your name, prepare for probate with your legal team, have the deceased's accounts and name changed from your auto and homeowners insurance.

Please do not delay in calling your financial advisor. If you do not have one or feel uncomfortable with the person or firm you are with, please feel free to call our firm. We handle estates and transfers on a regular basis. Call 888-647-1936 or 469-287-5657 (DFW local number).

❷ SOCIAL SECURITY OFFICE:

To claim survivor's benefits, you will need to contact them directly. Inform them of the deceased's name and SS number. Based on the age of the deceased, his work credits and any special considerations, they will assist you to determine what you are eligible for in the way of benefits.

❸ LIFE INSURANCE COMPANY:
(OFTEN YOUR AGENT WILL ASSIST YOU DIRECTLY WITH THESE CLAIMS)

<u>Individually Owned Policies</u> - Contact your insurance company, informing them that the policyholder is deceased. You will need to file a claim in order to receive your benefits. *The payout is not automatic.* This may also mean you need to call the deceased's employer if there was a company life insurance benefit. Both of these will request a certified copy of the Death Certificate to process this claim.

<u>Group Policies</u> - These can include employer, bank, credit agency, or other professional or social organizations. You will need to contact them to see if the deceased had a policy with them.

<u>Additional Policies</u> - Accidental Death and Dismemberment policy, Travel Accident insurance, Mortgage Life insurance, Car Payoff insurance, and Credit Life insurance to name a few.

NOTE THAT YOU DO HAVE OPTIONS ON HOW YOU TAKE YOUR PAYOUT, SO ASK YOUR FINANCIAL ADVISOR ABOUT THESE OPTIONS **BEFORE** CHOOSING ONE. FOR MORE INFORMATION ON INSURANCE SEE CHAPTERS 4 & 5.

❹ FUNERAL HOME, BURIAL AND/OR CREMATION:
For details on this section please turn to chapter 3.

❺ VETERAN'S ADMINISTRATION:
For more information on what they offer please turn to chapter's 3 & 11- look for this icon:

❻ LONG-TERM INSURANCE POLICY:
Notify them of the name of the deceased and cancel his policy. This insurance covers policyholders if they go into an assisted living or nursing home for the remainder of their life. If you are the spouse, you may be able to keep yourself insured; this usually will result in a lower premium.
(THIS TOPIC WILL BE COVERED MORE IN CHAPTER 5)

❼ MEDICARE SUPPLEMENT PLAN:

This insurance policy would assist with coverage for things that Medicare does not cover. If you are the spouse, you can opt to keep yourself insured; by removing the deceased from this policy, you will reduce your premium.

❽ ATTORNEY:

Notify them that your spouse has died, and they will start the process of getting the will probated. Have your attorney review the will and make an appointment to discuss any details.

❾ MINISTER AND/OR CHURCH:

If you plan to use a church or synagogue for your memorial service or funeral, you will need to contact them concerning these details. If you want a minister or priest to conduct the service, you will need to notify them of this as well.

> After the loss of a mate, it is very difficult to think clearly. You have so many things on your mind, and your emotions can make it difficult to function.
> Taking the time now to get a few things in place beforehand will greatly minimize the trauma of your loss.
> Death is not a pleasant thought, but it is inevitable. Wisely begin to prepare now.

Do not be overwhelmed by this list; divide and conquer if possible. Ask family, friends or your financial advisor to assist you in making some of these calls.

THE ONLY WAY TO TEST YOUR
LIMITS IS TO GO BEYOND THEM

Funerals & Other Details

Dan & Cindy's Story

I was never more grateful for Dan's attention to details than the days following his unexpected death.

A few years ago, Dan had a close friend die from cancer. His friend had had to make some tough decisions on details for his own funeral or cremation. That whole experience spurred Dan to arrange for our funerals in advance. I was very thankful for that wise decision as I found myself trying to deal with the grief of losing him.

The funeral home that Dan chose was wonderful to me and to our entire family. Their staff did everything they could to make this difficult time as easy for us as possible. As I reflect back, their compassion and concern was one bright spot in the middle of some very dark days. Dan had pre-paid for the majority of the funeral, saving me from having to deal with that added expense. I only had a few minor things to handle, and that was a blessing. In addition, I was so glad that Dan had expressed his wishes to them on many of the details involved in his funeral - things I would not have had the presence of mind to know how to choose. It was very comforting to me to know that he would have been pleased with every part of the service. It allowed me to have some closure, and for that I am very grateful.

John & Julie's Story

When John passed away, I wanted to make sure that his final wishes were met. One of his wishes was to be buried in the local Veterans' cemetery. I contacted the funeral home which had handled the service and burial of my mother a few year earlier. I explained my situation and set an appointment to meet with a funeral director. He was extremely helpful even though we had not pre-paid or even met with him prior to that day.

Fortunately, I was able to take Sue, a long time family friend, with me to help me make some of these difficult decisions. Since John was a veteran, there was no need to purchase a gravesite, which saved me some expense. And the Veterans Association even assisted us with the graveside service.

Even though we knew John was not well, I guess we just did not want to face the reality of his death by talking to a funeral home in advance. Waiting till John had passed made this a bit difficult, but the funeral home was very good to carefully walk me through each step, and in the end, it was not as bad as I had feared. But, as a result of this experience, I did opt to go ahead and make my own pre-paid funeral arrangements, in hopes of sparing my loved ones.

From Dr. Bill

Contacting the funeral home is one of the first phone calls you will need to make after a loved one dies, as indicated in chapter 2. If, like John and Julie, you do not have a pre-paid plan, deciding which funeral home to use is the first step. References from family and friends are a good way to locate one. Or you may need to simply visit several funeral homes and discuss with the funeral directors the different services and expenses, from the use of limousines, to flowers, the viewing and the actual service. Funerals can be very costly, and you will be making these decisions when you are emotional. Therefore, it would be wise to take a trusted friend or family member with you so they can help you make some of these decisions. If you are thinking of using some of the life insurance money for the funeral, be sure to discuss this with your financial advisor in advance so you know exactly how much you should plan to spend. You will also need to determine how you will pay for the services listed below. Will you pay with a credit card, check or cash? And how much can you realistically spend? Are you prepared to pay a partial amount, if not the full amount, for your package while at the funeral home or crematorium? Determine the answers to these questions before you move any further down this path.

OPTIONS - CHOOSE WHAT FITS YOU:
Funeral ■ Cremation ■ Organ/Whole Body Donation to Science

There are several options available if you have the luxury to investigate each one and determine which one you personally prefer. Having this decision made before your death will greatly reduce the stress on your loved ones. But if you find yourself facing these decisions on the heels of losing a loved one, proceed with wisdom and, again, seek wise counsel.

1. Funeral/Cremation Pre-paid Plan

If the deceased has a pre-paid plan, notify the funeral home of his name and inform them where they can pick up the body. Arrange for a meeting to discuss the remaining details of the funeral. You may still have a small fee due at the time of the funeral, covering any additional charges that were not originally included in your package.

2. Traditional Funeral/Cremation -No Prepaid Plan

Asking for referrals from friends and relatives is one way to sort through funeral homes. Once you have chosen the one you will use, contact them and arrange for the service, burial and/or cremation and any additional transportation of the body. Typically you will have multiple packages to choose from; *do not rush*, choose what bests fits your needs and budget. Pricing is important, but value and your satisfaction trumps everything else. Be aware of what packages may or may not include, such as visitation, the funeral or memorial service, cremation, casket, outer burial container, and/or cremation casket/urn. While cremation is becoming increasingly popular, it is not for everyone; take the time to cautiously consider all your options.

> **As in the case of a pre-paid funeral /cremation plan, arranging for either of these last two options in advance will greatly simplify things for your survivors.**

3. Crematorium

As I stated earlier, cremation is becoming increasingly popular. Some prefer it due to its lower cost, some for religious reasons, and still others because of their views about land use or environmental concerns.

If the deceased has a pre-paid plan, you will find a signed Authorization for Cremation form in their important documents. This will give you the name and contact number so you can notify them of his death and inform them where to pick up the body. It is important to know that crematoriums may or may not offer memorial service options. You may still need to schedule a service at your church or synagogue.

If the deceased has not pre-chosen a crematorium but has expressed that was his wish, you can search online for one in your area or ask a local funeral home or friend for a recommendation. You should inquire about the process of filing for a Death Certificate, and they should also arrange for transportation of the body to their facility.

4. Organ or Whole Body Donation to Science

There are many options available for those desiring to donate to science. You can contact a local teaching hospital, or there are several national organizations that you can contact via the web by doing an online search for "whole body donation". If the deceased was not pre-approved for donation, this will involve some paperwork along with a medical examination to determine if the body meets their criteria. Transportation fees may need to be paid for by the family, depending on the organization you choose. In addition, if a funeral home was utilized, there may be charges for their services. If the donor was pre-approved, you will find documentation in his important papers with the name of the organization and contact number. Notify them of the deceased's name and inform them where to pick up the body.

Death Certificate

The completion and submission of the death certificate forms to the Bureau of Vital Statistics is usually handled by the funeral home that will be overseeing the burial or cremation and is part of their fee. This will allow you to handle affairs such as settling the estate, collecting on a life insurance policy or terminating/receiving government services. To insure you have sufficient copies, we suggest anywhere from 10-15 be requested. If you find you need additional copies of the Death Certificate after it has been filed, you must contact the office in the state where your loved one died. Each state has its own requirements to obtain a copy of a Death Certificate. This information can be obtained online or by calling the office of Vital Statistics. There is a fee to obtain a Death Certificate from them. This fee varies from state to state.

There is some important information needed before the funeral home can file the death certificate. To make this process as stress-free as possible, you should have pertinent information on hand before proceeding to the funeral home.

Items Needed:

- Social Security Card (not just the SS number, to insure it is correct on the Death Certificate)
- Occupation at time of death
- Address, including county and zip code
- Marriage Certificate
- Surviving spouse's name
- Parent's names, including mother's maiden name
- If a Veteran - the DD-214 service documentation
- Place of burial, including cemetery section, lot and space
- If cremation is involved, or the body donated, this must also be noted

It is crucial to have this information at the time you go to the funeral home for two important reasons. First, it can delay filing of the death certificate if the information is not available. Second, if incorrect information is given, it will delay the process further, as an amended death certificate will need to be filed.

Obituary

Writing an obituary is one detail that often escapes even the most thorough planner. Writing an obituary for the funeral and/or publication (sometimes known as writing a funeral resolution) is another thing that can be taken care of in advance. At the very least having this information written down and filed with your important documents will be beneficial to your loved ones.

Obituary Format

The format that is usually followed for writing an obituary for a local newspaper is as follows:

- The name and address of the deceased
- The name and location of the hospital or city and state of the decedent's home
- Birth date, city and state where the person was born
- The person's mother and father may be listed if desired
- Schools that the person attended
- Memberships in any clubs or societies, as well as any honors they received
- A list of survivors, beginning with their spouse and children, then siblings and immediate family
- A list of immediate family members that predeceased the individual
- The name, address and phone number of the funeral home
- *Optional*: Time of wake and funeral, as well as the locations (*The reason it is optional is that there has been a rise in burglaries in homes during funeral services. If you do post this, we strongly suggest you have someone stay at the home during the service.*)

- The name of the individual who will be officiating at the ceremonies
- A list of where donations may be made in honor of the deceased

🖳 Visit **WWW.DRBILLCLARK.COM** and click on *The Next Step tab* to download the spreadsheet Important Personal Information.

Tips for Writing an Obituary

- Spell check the entire obituary before sending it to a newspaper.

- Make sure the person's name is spelled correctly. Surprisingly, this is the number one mistake.

- Avoid stating that a person died suddenly or unexpectedly. It is enough to write the date and location of where the person passed.

- Always include contact information so that obituary writers at the newspaper can reach you for clarification.

- Find out if there is an insertion fee for the obituary. This usually only applies if you are including a photo of the deceased or if you exceed a set number of words. Submitting an obituary without additional fees may delay when it will appear in the paper, so check on when it will be printed.

- Submitting an obituary to other papers, such as where the deceased grew up, is often appreciated by people who have fallen out of touch with them. Submitting one to the person's college alumni association or other associations such as lodges etc. where the person was a member is also appreciated. This gives fellow classmates or club members a chance to send condolences to the family.

Sample Obituary:

John T. Doe, died July 19, 2011, after a short illness. Born May 7, 1939 in Dripping Springs, TX he grew up and lived most of his working life in the Dallas metroplex. He moved to Plano, Tx in August, 1995. In 1967, along with his sister June, he established a small mail order business for gourmet coffees. The family enterprise took its name, Dumas Inc., from their beloved family dog of many years. Local residents occasionally joined the frenzied family each year as the holiday season approached. Their small business would be filled with shipping boxes and the aroma of coffee would pervaded the small corporate building. Under the philosophy of "Better Beans make a Better Brew," the small company flourished and developed a nationwide customer base. The next generation of Doe's has now taken over, but John's enthusiastic spirit continues. Surviving are his son, John Doe, Jr. and wife, Nancy, of McKinney, Tx; daughter, Janice Doe Thomas and husband, George; and five grandchildren, Joseph Thomas, Matt Thomas, Lucy Thomas Medlin, Timothy Thomas and Tracey Thomas Kelty. The memorial service will be held at 11:00 am, Friday, July 25 at Plano Presbyterian Church with the Reverend Lincoln, officiating. Memorials may be made to Hospice of Plano, Inc., 1122 Main Street, Anywhere, USA 12345.

 **Veteran Information**

If you or your spouse served in the military, you will want to look into these benefits. These benefits will not be paid automatically. Claims for Veterans' benefits must usually be made within two years from the date of final interment.

Death and Memorial Benefits

Your family may qualify for veterans' death benefits for honorably discharged veterans in the event of your own death or that of your spouse:

- Headstone or Marker
- $300 Burial expense (certain circumstances, if qualified)
- $150 plot or interment allowance (certain circumstances, if qualified)
- US flag (most cases)
- Burial in national cemetery (spouse usually included)
- Internment in Columbarium at Arlington National Cemetery, Arlington, VA, is free for the veteran (spouse usually included)

These are not all-inclusive, as the costs for a casket or urn, services of the funeral directory and transportation of the body are typically not covered. The value of the benefit varies according to locale but may be as much as $10,000 if the goods and services were purchased on the consumer market. Some VA assistance may be available for burial elsewhere, depending on service periods. The spouse or un-remarried surviving spouse of an eligible veteran is also eligible for burial in a national cemetery. Minor children of an eligible veteran may also be buried in a national cemetery. For specifics, call your local Veterans Administration Office.

To File A Claim for Veteran's Benefits

The following forms must be submitted:

- Veteran's discharge papers
- Certified copy of Death Certificate
- Copy of Marriage Certificate
- Birth Certificate of minor children
- Receipted itemized funeral bill

Other VA Benefits

Benefits for orphans and widows of veterans vary, but look into what is available in your case.

- Burial in national cemeteries
- Burial expense reimbursement
- Burial flag for veterans (obtain at Post Office)
- Compensation for widows and orphans
- Pension for widows and minor children
- Parent's compensation
- Children's education - for children of veterans whose death was service-connected or who were 100% disabled
- Home loans for widows or unremarried widows of veterans who die of service-connected causes are eligible for G.I. Home Loans
- Headstone or grave marker
- Emergency financial aid for needy widows
- Real estate tax exemption for needy unremarried widows of veterans who were 100% disabled

THE JOURNEY OF LIFE OFFERS
MANY CHOICES!

Investments

William & Ruth's Story

When it came to our investments, I was not sure where to begin after William passed away. William and I had occasionally used a financial advisor over the past several years; William sometimes referred to him as our broker. Anyway, I decided to called his office to get his advice and ask some questions about our investments. I wanted to know if the remaining funds would be sufficient to sustain me for the remainder of my life.

Over the phone, our advisor instructed me to gather up the last three months of statements from all of our accounts, including our bank accounts and brokerage accounts. I was to bring all of these things to our meeting later that week. Finding each of these things was not difficult. Funny how time can change your view of things; I used to think William was a bit too organized, but on that day I was thanking God for his detailed organization. I also realized how fortunate I was to have been familiar with our filing system, partly because I had occasionally handled our bills. I have played golf over the years with other girls who did not know a thing about their finances or bills; they would have been lost.

The advisor reviewed the investments in light of my new financial standing as a widow. He mentioned that since William was no longer going to be the one making the investment decisions, it was his suggestion that he take up that role. He said he would get back with me in a few days with his findings.

A few days later, a friend was visiting with me, and the subject of my financial standing and my investments came up. He recommended that I get a second opinion on my investments before changing any of them. He gave me the name of his broker who dealt primarily with people in the retirement phase of life. As it turned out, it was a good decision to "shop around," I discovered that not every broker has experience with clients who are retired. My needs dictated a different set of investment priorities. After talking with several brokers, I was able to find one that had experience with retired clients and was willing to explain things to me. If I had not looked into our investments with someone who understood my situation, I might not have been able to sustain my present life style. Any radical swings in the market could have reduced my needed income, and at this stage of life, that could be catastrophic. Looking back now, I realize I was lucky to find an informed advisor.

From Dr. Bill

You should consult with more than one financial advisor about your investments. There is not a "one-size-fits-all" in this field. Each one will have varying strengths and objectives - some are more concerned with accumulation instead of preservation. As seen in the story above, at the retirement stage of life, preservation is the most important thing. Finding a conservative registered investment advisor who specializes in retirement planning is critical. This advisor will not actually sell stocks or bonds or even mutual funds, meaning they will not profit directly from your decisions, but are there to give sound advice. Investment advisors typically work on a fee basis.

When an advisor looks at your investments, he should carefully consider your overall investment mix. A quality investment advisor or broker can develop an investment portfolio that will provide quality income and growth for this new season of life. In addition, they should also consider the tax implications of the investments that you hold. Some investments are tax free - others are not. A good advisor will give sound counsel concerning decisions on whether to continue to hold on to stocks and bonds or to liquidate them and invest them elsewhere.

Think long term when it comes to investing. I know it can be exciting to check the value of your portfolio every day, particularly since doing this is easy, thanks to the internet. But micro-managing your investments in this way can lead you to make emotion-based decisions depending on the way the wind is blowing in the markets that day. Some investments, such as fixed-index annuity, may not make substantial profits but are able to weather the seasons of an unstable market. It may sound strange, but zero profit in a bad market is actually good, so do not let emotions drive your investment decisions.

As seen in Ruth's story, her age needed to play a part in the decisions an advisor would make. A good advisor understands that as his clients advance in age, their ability to recover from a major financial downturn is limited. In recent years we have seen two 40% drops in the market which have forced many retirees back into the work force just to support themselves. Many retirees found themselves in this position even after diligently investing in seemingly sound plans. Many were invested in 401(k) plans and retirements plans whose value dropped significantly over the last ten to twelve years.

Another factor to consider when dealing with investments are qualified or non-qualified investments. For example, some accounts such as IRA's, 401(k)'s, and 403(b)'s are qualified accounts - meaning that the principal and interest in most cases has not been taxed, so any withdrawal from those accounts would have to be declared as income. Non-qualifying accounts have principal that has already been taxed but perhaps the growth in the account has not been taxed. How you will be taxed, based on your investment choices needs to be factored into the overall decision.

If you are considering annuities, you need to obtain them from someone who understands the tax consequences. If your annuity has not been written correctly, you are in danger of paying an excessive amount of tax. There are different kinds of annuities for different purposes. An immediate annuity can generate a lifetime retirement income. With the immediate annuity, you deposit a sum with an annuity company, which in turn will pay you a monthly amount for life or a lesser amount to continue over the life of both you and your spouse.

Immediate annuities can be treated as an exempt asset if you need to qualify for Medicaid. These payments can also cover long term care needs or premiums. Another advantage is that most of the income can be tax-free and provides more income than other conservative investments. However, if you die early, not only does the income end, but also the annuity company keeps the remaining funds. This does keep some investors away from this kind of annuity. There are a few companies who will guarantee the remaining funds to your heirs with "life payments with refund."

The advisor you choose should also evaluate your present investment portfolio to determine whether you are making money or losing money. Your financial situation should be more important than his own commissions. Finally, a quality advisor will ask a wide range of open-ended questions to help him determine what is best for you in your current situation. Please read the sample questions on the next page. If your advisor is not asking these questions, I suggest you look into securing a new advisor.

Sample Questions:

♦ What is important to you about your money?

♦ What are your monthly expenses? What is your new monthly income?

♦ Are there annual or semi–annual expenses that you pay?

♦ What do you want your money to do for you?

♦ What are your dreams or goals (travel for example) that you would like to seek?

♦ What legacy would you like to leave in your deceased spouse's name or your name? This could be for a church, school, hospital, or other non-profit organization.

♦ Who is asking you for money? Who might ask in the near future? What do you want to do about it?

♦ What is your greatest fear about the money you have?

"WE HAVE A VERY STRATEGIC
APPROACH TO INVESTING."

Insurance, What to Make of it All

Roger & Claire's Story

I found myself sitting alone in our darkened office crying. How did I get into this mess? I am a smart woman, I ran an office in my younger years. But for some reason I found myself completely puzzled by the financial papers I was trying to organize. Over the years, Roger had requested many times that I take the time to learn these things - but I never seemed to find the time. I always thought that I would "get around to it" one day, but that day never came.

I sat looking at our checkbook and bank statements, trying to understand the various premiums being paid to our car insurance, long term care insurance, Medicare supplement insurance, life insurance and annuities. I was at a total loss to understand if these figures were correct or if they should be different now that Roger was deceased. I was dealing with a gamut of emotions, wondering if I still needed some of these policies like the long-term care insurance, and based on the figures I was seeing on these papers, I was not even sure if I could afford them.

I was fortunate because Roger and I had found a great financial advisor a few years prior to Roger's passing. He had assisted us on many occasions, and I trusted his insight. I gathered up my paperwork and decided that I needed to get his counsel on this matter. Without a moment's thought,

I got in my car and drove over to his office. I walked in, held out the papers, and with tears running down my face, I asked if he could make any sense of these insurance papers. I look back now and realize that I must have been a complete mess, but he never said one word about my appearance. He simply took them from my hand, pulled up a chair for me and quietly handed me a box of tissue. Over the next forty minutes, he patiently walked me through each of the policies and premiums that I was paying.

As it turns out, it was a good thing I asked for his advice. There were a few policies that I could cancel, but a few of them had serious issues. Thankfully, with his help we got each of the issues resolved, and I was back to feeling confident about my ability to both understand and deal with these insurance policies. I found that having the right person to advise you is as important as realizing you need help. My advisor was compassionate and willing to explain things in a manner I could understand and helped me to logically see what I needed to do. His advice not only helped me, but I have been able to pass along some of his helpful insights to my friends.

From Dr. Bill
Filing for a life insurance claim after the death of a loved one can be difficult, but to receive payment, you must notify the insurance company of the person's passing. Many insurance companies today will send an actual checkbook for payout on larger policies, instead of a one time check. The recipients are instructed to write checks to cover expenses or to pay off any debts. In theory this allows the family time to deal with their loss and take their time deciding what to do with the insurance money while offering an easy way to pay for expenses. The insurance company typically informs the family that the funds are in an interest-bearing account that you can access at any time. It is important to note that the insurance company continues collecting additional interest on this amount until all the funds are withdrawn.

Some people are not comfortable with the insurance companies benefiting from the death of a loved one and opt to cash out the entire balance immediately while others like the ease of the checkbook over dealing with a large sum. Some companies may offer options on the insurance payouts from a single lump sum to payments over the course of your life. Bottom line, do not hesitate to ask questions concerning your payout options.

It is always wise to examine each of your policies from time to time and see if they need to be adjusted based on your present situation. Taking time to really look at what you are presently paying and what you now need could reduce your premium. An insurance premium is the actual amount of money charged by insurance companies for active coverage.

You might also consider looking at other insurance providers for a better price or coverage. An insurance premium for the same service can vary widely among insurance providers. That is why I advise you to get several quotes before committing to an insurance policy. Do not simply look at the cost of the coverage, also look at the amount of coverage you will be receiving. In the case of car insurance, your age, type of vehicle, where you live, how many vehicles you own and what kind of coverage you want will all affect the quotes you will receive.

Medical insurance rates can also vary based on if the insured is a non-smoker verses smoker, what his age is, if there is any serious medical history and more. When you cancel the insurance for the deceased, look into the remaining policies to insure you have adequate coverage.

Another type of insurance is based on annuities. An annuity is an investment vehicle sold primarily by insurance companies. Several types of annuities exist. Every annuity has two basic properties: whether the payout is immediate or deferred and whether the returns are fixed or variable. An annuity with immediate payout begins payments to the annuitant immediately after it is purchased, while deferred payout means that the investor will receive payment at some later date. An annuity with a fixed return offers guarantees from the insurance companies. An annuity with a variable return offers results that vary with the performance of the variable investments such as mutual funds, but the account value is not guaranteed. This means that the money is invested in the securities market. If the securities market is going up, then most likely that account value goes up. If the securities market goes down, so will the account. Be aware that variable annuities usually have high fees. These can be avoided with a fixed or fixed-index annuity.

Most annuities are either designed for income or for investment growth. A qualified investment advisor would know the different types of annuities and what would be best for you. There is a famous financial planner who was asked, "My advisor is recommending that I put my retirement account in a variable annuity. What should I do?" To which he responded "Run, and get yourself another financial advisor!"

List of Various Types of Insurance:

Car Insurance - There are two types of coverage.

- **COLLISION COVERAGE** will pay to have your vehicle repaired in the event of an accident. This coverage will most likely have a deductible (the amount you must pay out of pocket).

- **LIABILITY COVERAGE** will pay to settle a claim of the other person if you are at fault in an accident. It is VERY important that your liability limits are substantial enough to meet a high claim against you.

Home Owner's Insurance - This is coverage that covers your home, the contents of your home, and liability brought against you if someone is injured at your home.

Umbrella Liability Insurance - This type of coverage attaches to your homeowner's and car insurance for additional liability coverage usually beginning at $1,000,000.

Long Term Care Insurance - This is coverage that will assist in covering the ever-increasing cost of home health care, assisted living, and nursing home care. There are several types of coverages. Recently a new coverage for LTC has been approved that is tied to a life insurance policy. This may substantially reduce the cost of the insurance.

Life Insurance - This will pay upon the death of the insured. It can be used to pay final expenses, income tax on IRAs and 401Ks, and even pay federal estate taxes if set up correctly

Medicare Supplement - This coverage will pay the cost of medical and hospital coverage that Medicare part A and part B do not cover.

Medicare Part D - This is the insurance for prescription drugs. It is required by Medicare even if you do not take any prescription drugs.

"NOT ALL INSURANCE COMPANIES
TAKE YOUR MONEY AND RUN."

Income & Cash Flow

Frank & Elaine's Story

After Frank passed, I struggled with the magnitude of the things that were now altered for me forever, one being that I was now in charge of our finances. This was never something I felt comfortable doing. I had on occasions been with Frank when he paid the bills, dealt with Social Security or went to bat for our medical coverage. But deep down, I hoped that I would never have to deal with this on my own.

Now I had to finally face the music; I was not only in charge, I was totally confused. I knew that our income from Social Security would be reduced because Frank was no longer living. But I found it rather funny, tongue-in-cheek, that my expenses never went down because he was gone. I was still paying the same rent, water, gas and electricity along with various premiums and more. But that aside, I was confused with the Social Security checks as they began arriving shortly after his death. I did not understand how they came to this new amount. I did not know if this new amount would be my regular income now or if it would change again in the future.

Add to my confusion the fact that I was now trying to figure up all my bills and calculate how to make sure I had enough to cover them - with this reduced income. I had to create a list of bills and chart out when these bills were due and then see when various checks would be deposited in my account. Some were once a month; some were less often than that. In addition, I was also trying to make sense of other funds that were deposited into our joint account from our brokerage firm. I could not tell if these were in fact a set amount or if they varied from month to month. All of these things made it next to impossible for me to try to determine any form of budget.

Despite my apprehension, I attempted to put down on paper all my expenses, along with the estimated income, and tried to see if I had enough to cover my monthly expenses. When I was all finished, I thought that my income level would be sufficient. But I decided that I needed to get a second opinion. I set an appointment with our financial advisor and hoped he could clear it all up for me.

That was the smartest decision I made, and it saved me considerable frustration in the long run. He began to explain to me that while I was figuring my known monthly expenses correctly, I was not including any additional funds that I might need in the case of unplanned emergencies. What if my car broke down, or I was to suddenly become ill, or one of my grandkids needed financial aid; I was not setting aside any additional funds for these rainy-day needs.

In addition, I was unclear if these funds came into my account by direct deposit or if I should be getting regular checks, nor did I know when these funds should arrive. These few details were critical for me to understand so I would not be caught off guard with more bills and needs than I had funds to cover. I cannot tell you how much better I slept once I did get all these things cleared up and accounted for. I was fortunate; after all the accounting was done, I did have enough regular funds to cover all the bills, including some emergency money. But I could have been in a pickle if I had not had someone help me get this all set up and calculated.

From Dr. Bill

If you and your spouse are on Social Security and you report the passing of your spouse, in most cases the Social Security Administration will recalculate the social security and continue the largest amount. In some rare cases the surviving spouse is not eligible to receive Social Security. The Social Security Administration will advise you of this when you contact them. When Social Security is approved, I recommend that it be set up for direct deposit into your bank account. This will prevent theft from the mail box.

Calculating your revised monthly budget can be overwhelming. But with the right help, you can get a plan in place that will insure all your bills will be paid on time and that you will have enough for those unexpected things as well. Elaine realized that she needed to have all her checks moved to direct deposit and get as many of her monthly expenses on scheduled payments, reducing the things she would have to attend to on a monthly basis. She needed help in getting all these details in order, but once she did, maintaining it was simple.

Budget

Begin by getting your check book, bank statements or bills that are coming in and determine which are regular, ongoing expenses. These may be the utilities like electric, water and sewage, phone, cable or satellite bills. Make a list of these expenses. Next, look at your food and entertainment expenses. These can vary each month. Finally write down your mortgage, taxes, and home & car insurance cost. These are your necessary budget items. Please note, your taxes and insurance may only bill once a year. Be sure to withhold 1/12 of these expenses each month so that you will have money to pay them at the time of billing.

For your convenience, we have included a link on our website where you can download helpful spreadsheets that will assist you in making a budget.  Visit **WWW.DRBILLCLARK.COM** and click on *The Next Step tab*.

DON'T TRIP OVER DOLLARS
TO PICK UP PENNIES

Debt, What Do You Owe?

Sue & Sam's Story

When my husband Sam passed away, I found myself in a financially sticky situation. Over the span of our 40 years of marriage we had acquired a large sum of debt. I was aware of this debt but just assumed that by the time we were going to retire we would have most of that whittled down. I was wrong. Losing Sam while he was still working caught me totally by surprise. He had been sick, but we never dreamed he would die from his medical issues. His unexpected death was heart wrenching, but having to then deal with all the financial decisions, mainly the amount of debt we had, was just as difficult for me.

Shortly after Sam passed away, I asked a close friend for the name of a trusted individual who could help me with my finances. I realized that without Sam's salary, paying my monthly bills was now going to be difficult even with his life insurance. I contacted the gentleman who was recommended and scheduled an appointment. I began to gather the papers he had requested for our first meeting. Thankfully, I was very familiar with paying bills and understood where we kept all of our important papers and documents. Sam and I had always shared this part of our life, but as I began to really look at the size of our debt in light of my situation, I began to panic. I realized that without Sam's income I was way over my head financially.

We not only had a large mortgage on our home but both our cars were new; we had not paid cash for them. In addition, over the years, we had signed for college loans for our grandchildren. The full realization of these monthly bills began to press in on me, and I felt the room begin to spin. Unfortunately, I was not at the end of the debt total yet. Next, I began to pull out the credit card statements, and I realized our debt was substantial here as well partly due to some of the medical expenses we had incurred prior to Sam's passing. There were department store cards and major credit cards, and each had a monthly payment that now seemed staggeringly large. I was quickly spiraling into a dark emotional hole. I remember going to bed that night and feeling a real loss in my heart, loss of a husband and lover, loss of a life that we had lived, and loss of any naivety that it would all be okay because Sam was still working.

Facing these hard facts with my financial advisor was not pleasant, but he was able to give me wise counsel on how to reduce my debt down to a manageable size. He walked me through evaluating what debt I still owed and how much life insurance benefit I would be receiving. Then he helped me add this amount to my current investments. Next we looked at refinancing my home, refinancing the credit card debt which was set at a very high interest rate and selling at least one of our cars. All this would help to get me out from under the monthly burden that I was facing. Because of my age, a reverse mortgage was not one that he was willing to suggest to me just yet; it would only be a last resort if necessary to pay off all of the high-interest debt. It was a sobering realization for me to undertake all these decisions on my own. The mounds of paperwork and details were overwhelming to me. But I did not have a choice; I had to get on top of this debt or it would bury me as well.

The months following Sam's passing were very painful. I was not only dealing with the loss of my husband, but now I was also having to make some major decisions that would affect my present and future lifestyle. If only we had been more aware of our debt sooner, if only...

52

From Dr. Bill

From Sue's story you see how important it is to get on top of your debt before you are faced with a sudden loss. But even if you are facing the same situation as Sue, you can begin to reduce your debt with some basic steps.

Begin by reviewing debt; it is important to determine when the bills are due and to set up your cash flow to have money to pay these bills each week. Look at your total debt: mortgage, auto, college loans, credit cards, and any others.

Next, determine what the balance and the interest rates are on each of these items of your debt. Then look at the pay-off date at your current rate of payment. If possible, develop an accelerated payment plan in order to pay off all the high-interest debt first. Set an attainable goal or target date in order to have each of the credit cards and high-interest debts paid off. For your convenience we have included a link on our website where you can download a Balance Sheet. This spreadsheet will help you to determine your total assets and liabilities. Visit **WWW.DRBILLCLARK.COM** and click on *The Next Step tab*.

It is also possible to reduce or totally eliminate some if not all of your debt by negotiation with your creditors. I recommend that you find an expert to advise you, but do not pay them in advance. There are some companies that will charge you $6,000 to $8,000 in order to negotiate your debt, but in many cases you can be just as successful as they are if you have good counsel on how to negotiate with them.

"DISCIPLINE IS THE BRIDGE
BETWEEN GOALS AND
ACCOMPLISHMENTS."

Legal Documents

Clyde & Helen's Story

When my husband Clyde passed away, I had my eyes opened to the importance of correct legal documentation. I found myself facing several different legal concerns that I was unprepared to handle on my own.

First, I wrongly assumed that since Clyde had his Power of Attorney papers indicating that I could act on his behalf that I would be able to use this same power after he was gone. But I found out that was not the case at all. As a result, I was informed that Clyde's will had to be probated. I knew very little about what that meant or how to begin the process. Even though I was exhausted, I needed to get this resolved. So I turned on the computer and got online to see what I needed to do. I learned that this had to be done by a court in order to transfer the title of his assets to me. I also learned that since our cars and home were jointly owned, I could simply retitle them in my name. But probating his will was not quite as simple. I quickly discovered that I was way out of my league. With the help of a close friend, I located a good probate attorney. This attorney informed me that this process varies from state to state, but in either case it was imperative to get the will probated as soon as possible and that he would be willing to see to that for me.

That got me thinking about all my other legal documents. I realized that many of them needed to be reviewed in light of Clyde's passing. The first document that I wanted to address was my will. I located it in our fireproof box and found that, just as I suspected, Clyde was listed as my executor and the beneficiary of my assets. Since Clyde was no longer living, I knew that this needed to be changed. I since have learned that we could have listed a substitute executor and/or independent representative in addition to Clyde, but we had neither. So once again I found myself in need of advice and counsel. I wanted to ensure that my children and various charities were listed as my beneficiaries in the event of my death.

All I wanted to do just then was rewind the clock and make Clyde be there in the room with me to advise me on what to do. The reality of how alone I really was began to sink in. But once again I contacted the attorney and set up another appointment.

After we had discussed the will and completed all the important changes, the lawyer brought up another concern. He mentioned that my Durable Power of Attorney of finances or assets also had only Clyde's name on it, as did my Medical Power of Attorney. These had been drafted years ago, giving Clyde the ability to oversee my affairs in case I was unable to or incapable of managing them any longer. The reality that I now needed to find a new person to fill that role caught me off guard. I needed to really give this some serious thought. I had been married to Clyde for many years and trusted him completely. I never once questioned giving him that kind of power, but handing this to someone else was a different story. I was unprepared to make that decision right then, so I asked the lawyer if I could be back in touch with him after a few days. There was so much to try to process and consider while dealing with the emotional devastation of losing Clyde. Strangely, this was like the last straw for me; I found myself hitting a wall emotionally. I was overwhelmed at the reality that Clyde was not going to ever be there to take care of me. I almost felt like I was losing him all over again.

The lawyer was very understanding, and he gave me some advice on how to come to this decision. Seeing that I was ready to bolt from the office, he quickly mentioned that at some point I needed to examine my life insurance, IRA and retirement accounts as well - to see if they also listed Clyde as the sole beneficiary. If so, then if I were to die, all of these would go into my estate and could undergo substantial taxation before being given to my heirs. The attorney recommended a couple of financial advisors to visit.

I was in such a fog leaving his office that afternoon. I barely remember the drive home or that evening. But by the next day I was feeling more clearheaded and was able to begin the process of making these decisions. It took me weeks to get each one of these revised, but with the help of family, friends and good counsel I was finally able to get all my documents in order.

From Dr. Bill

When you experience the loss of a loved one, it is emotionally devastating. It can be very difficult to think clearly at such a vulnerable time. That is why it is important to get quality legal counsel for your wills, trusts, and Powers of Attorney, when this happens. At the very least, have these documents reviewed by a competent attorney so that he or she can give you good counsel on how to set up or rewrite them in light of the death.

There is another document called a Revocable Living Trust that you might consider. This document would allow your assets to transfer outside of probate in the event of your passing. Many couples set these up so that the surviving spouse will not have probate at the passing of the first spouse. The Revocable Living Trust can be complicated, but many people use them to avoid probate. If probate is a difficult issue in your state, then I would seek legal counsel on the benefits of this type of legal document to protect your assets in probate. Typically, a Revocable Living Trust will not protect assets from a lawsuit, but it can minimize legal costs in the event of death of a spouse

Living Will Information

A living will is a legal paper in which you spell out your desire for care if you have a terminal medical condition or are in a state of complete incapacity or permanent unconsciousness.

With a living will you express, while you are in good health, your rational choice of when to discontinue life support. Most importantly, you decide the precise circumstances for discontinuing treatment and also clearly state whom among your loved ones and healthcare providers should have the power to decide when to withdraw life support. Most states have laws that say living wills are legal. Many doctors will honor living wills even in a state without a living will law.

Power of Attorney (P.O.A.) Information

A Durable Power of Attorney for Health Care Decisions allows you (the principal) to name another person (the attorney-in-fact) to make certain medical decisions for you if you are unable to make them for yourself.

The Law says that the attorney-in-fact can:

- Authorize your admission to a medical, nursing, residential or other facility
- Enter into agreements for your care
- Authorize medical and surgical procedures

The power to "authorize medical and surgical procedures" means that your attorney-in-fact may arrange for and consent to medical, therapeutic, and surgical procedures for you, including the administration of drugs. Consult with an attorney to prepare a P.O.A. for Health Care Decisions.

Unlike a living will, you do not have to be in a terminal condition or permanent state of unconsciousness, for your attorney-in-fact to act on your behalf. If it is unclear if your representative under a P.O.A. for health care can refuse or stop sustaining treatment for you, your living will can clearly be used for that purpose.

Things to Consider:

- Is your will up to date?
- Have the beneficiaries changed?
- Has your executor or executrix changed?
- Do you need to change your Power of Attorney for Finances and Health?
- If you are using a Revocable Living Trust, does it need revision?
- Are you satisfied with your Directive to Physicians also known as a Living will?
- Who is listed on your HIPPA form to have access to your medical records? (HIPPA - HEALTH INSURANCE PORTABILITY AND ACCOUNTABILITY)
- Have you discussed guardianship with your children?
- Is it important to you that you DO NOT want to disinherit your GRANDCHILDREN? If the answer is yes then consider having your beneficiaries changed by adding the phrase "per-stirpes" after your children's name. This legal phrase will allow your assets to pass from your children to your grandchildren in the event of pre-mature death of your child or children. If you have questions, please ask a qualified advisor or an attorney.

"YES, MA'AM, WE HAVE ONE OF THE BEST WARRANTIES IN THE INDUSTRY."

Taxes

Betty's Story

I am a retired, divorced/single woman, who relied upon several qualified professionals to help me get to the place that I could retire comfortably. One of those professionals was my CPA, whom I used for over 15 years. I had never had any complaints with his accounting, but on a whim one day, I decided to ask my financial advisor to look over my taxes just to see if everything was in order. This ended up being an excellent decision on my part.

It came to my attention that my CPA was not as current on investments and subsequent taxes as my financial advisor was. He brought to my understanding that I had a substantial amount of dividend and interest income, $15,000 a year. I was not living on this income, but was reinvesting it each year. He informed me that with my current arrangement, I was being taxed on that amount as if I were living on it. That explained the high tax rate that I had been paying each year which was well over $5,000. I had always wondered if that rate was right, but I blindly assumed that my CPA was doing the best he could to get me the best tax rates. I was frustrated that I had been paying this amount for years.

My financial advisor asked me if he could reallocate the principal in my dividend investments and instead allow them to grow with different vehicles. I did decide to do this small adjustment to my accounting. By doing this I would avoid declaring them as income each year. That one act lowered my taxes by $3,000 - which I was, of course, thrilled about. That gave me the funds to do something I had been wanting to do for some time: take my grand kids to Disneyworld. My only regret is that I did not have him evaluate my taxes sooner.

Ed & Rose's Story

We learned a good lesson about taxes one year when our financial advisor began to look into our CD that was reinvested every year. We were living off of the interest that came from that CD, and so as a result we had always paid taxes on that interest.

He suggested a different plan for our funds that were in the CD, moving them into two short-term annuities. One guaranteed income for five years, and the other annuity was left to grow for that same five years. By doing this we received the exact same amount that we had been getting on our CD, but now we were only taxed on a small fraction of that sum. Overall, it lowered our taxes by $1,000. Who wouldn't be excited with the idea of paying less in taxes? We were very thankful that he was so attentive to our investments; left to our own, we would still be giving that $1,000 to Uncle Sam.

From Dr. Bill

As in the stories above, you see that many tax accountants or even CPAs are recording history in your tax returns - i.e. your profits, your losses, your income, and your deductions; they may not be trained to look at strategies that reduce your taxes in the future. As a result you might continue to pay those same tax rates not knowing that there could be other options.

In Betty's case, merely redirecting her existing investments allowed her to not be taxed until she elected to pay the tax. That saved her $4,000 a year over a ten year period that is a $40,000 savings. That is the cost of a new car or paying off a home. She was free to redirect that money to anything she wanted. This was income that was unnecessarily falling between the cracks.

In many cases, like Ed and Rose, by using an immediate income/deferral strategy, we can develop a guaranteed income for the rest of their lives while only paying income tax on a very small part of that sum.

Tax planning can help you legally lower your income tax and increase the return on your investments by making interest on your principal, interest on the interest, and interest on the tax saving. This small strategy can make you thousands of dollars over a lifetime.

In addition, you may be eligible for an exemption on your taxes as a widow or widower, depending on how long your spouse has been deceased and whether you have remarried. It's important you choose the best option because your filing status determines your tax rate and standard deduction, with one option saving you the most money. These options are available for 2 years after the death of your spouse. While your mate was alive, you had two incomes and income taxes were withheld from both social security and/or pensions. Now that you are a widow or widower you have less taken out of your income (note that you may need to increase that amount so you don't have to pay additional taxes). With this decrease of income, the IRS allows you to claim this exempt status for two years after your spouse has passed. Your accountant or CPA can elect the widow or widower's exemption which allows you most of their exemption during those two years until you can get back on your feet.

"YOU REALLY HAVEN'T LOST ANY MONEY...YOUR ACCOUNT IS JUST WORTH LESS NOW."

Family & Their Financial Needs

Mary Ann's Story

You may have heard it said that money and death do strange things to families, and sadly I found that to be true. Glen and I were married nearly 20 years when he was killed in an car accident. We had both been married before, and we each had children from our previous marriages. Blending our family was not an issue for us since we married long after the kids were out on their own. Because of that, before Glen passed away, I had always thought that I had a great relationship with his son, Marcus, but after Glen was gone, things began to change.

Marcus had always struggled to find his way in the world and was continuously just barely making it financially. He had been in and out of many jobs, never seeming to find a good fit for him. There were plenty of excuses for each of the jobs he left or was released from, but the pattern revealed that it was a deeper issue with him. Over the years he had hinted to Glen that he could sure use some financial help, but Glen never gave more than a few hundred dollars at any given time. When we drew up our will, he purposely left each of the kids the same amount, not favoring him despite his need - but Glen expressed his hope that Marcus would use his portion to help him get out of his financial mess.

The inheritance Glen left to each of the children was a sizeable amount. It could have allowed Marcus to purchase a small home and buy a used but newer car, and possibly even pay off a few of his debts. I was so hopeful that this would give him the boost he needed to then focus on finding a full time job and getting back on his feet. But these funds ended up not really helping Marcus like we had hoped.

It started with Marcus' thinking that he was somehow shorted in the inheritance. He began to make statements that he had gotten less than his sister, even though he knew that they both got the same amount. Then he became more hostile toward me, and within a few short months after Glen died, Marcus approached me, strongly demanding that I give him additional funds out of the inheritance I had received. As it turned out, the home he wanted was larger than his money would cover, and the car he had already purchased was a very expensive luxury vehicle and was more than he could really afford. Both of these choices perpetuated his bad financial state. When I tried to ask him for explanations, he was full of excuses and blame. He felt I was at fault for a lot of things, most of which I had no control over. I was torn about what to do. I knew that he had not used the funds well, and giving him more would not really solve the real problem, but at the same time, it was his father who had died. I was conflicted; I really wanted to do the right thing.

Marcus began to call or drop by my home on a daily basis. He would make statements about Glen's being his father and that if I had not married him, he would have gotten a larger portion of Glen's inheritance. He would then proceed to plead for me to pay off a bill that was due or cover an expense that he had. I had no one to turn to for support or advice. I was still dealing with the loss of Glen, making my emotions more vulnerable. I was so beaten down by his constant requests that finally I decided to just give him some money in hopes that this would put an end to the whole thing. By doing so, I knew that I was cutting my own funds and jeopardizing my own future, but I rationalized that I could cut back a few places and make do. Deep down, what I really wanted was for Marcus to stop hounding me.

He seemed genuinely grateful for the money at the time, and so far he has not asked for more; but then it has only been a few months. He has at least stopped calling me, for which I am grateful. If he does come back asking for more, I am going to get a third party individual to help me deal with him. I hate to resort to that, but I feel it is my only option.

James & Susan's Story

Susan and I have served in the ministry for many years. That lifestyle was not lavish, but we were very frugal and always content with what we had. We had a friend who had helped us years ago with our few investments, so while we did not have much, we had managed to retire with a small savings. In addition we had paid off our single car and modest-sized home, which was a tight fit when the kids were underfoot but was just right for us as we became less active and climbed up in years.

As we were approaching our 70's, our daughter and son-in-law asked us to move across the country to live with them. They wanted to help relieve us of some of financial demands of life and care for us. The house sold quickly, and we packed up and moved in with them. Shortly after moving in, our son-in-law approached us about using some of the funds we got from the sale of the house to pay for an addition to be added to their home - this addition would give us our own mother-in-law suite. We thought that was a great idea and gave them $100,000. It was a huge fortune to us and the majority of our savings. But we rationalized that this was allowing us to live out the remainder of our days in comfort and we were investing in real estate.

One year later, our son-in-law informed us that his business had not been making money for over a year, and that the bank would be foreclosing on the home within the month. We were so stunned that we were speechless. All of our investment was now gone - and we had no way to get it back. Susan and I were devastated. This hit us on several levels. Not only had we lost a large portion of our savings, but we felt a deep betrayal from our family. They never once let on that there were any financial concerns; they pretended that life was fine and continued to eat out and live like nothing was wrong until the day the bank took it all away.

From Dr. Bill

When money, death and family issues are mixed, it can be a combustible combination. As in Mary Ann's story, the inheritance, while intended to be a blessing, backfired and even caused some pain to the loved ones left behind. I have seen children of every age mishandle the wealth left to them. Many estate disputes are ignited by seeds of jealousy, greed, and hurt feelings. Such feelings can erupt into actions that can permanently damage relationships. Unfortunately, age does not dictate maturity nor does calamity create character, but it will reveal it.

One form that can be beneficial when dividing up possessions is a Personal Property Disposition. This is a written statement, referenced to in a will, that is used to dispose of items of tangible personal property that are not specifically disposed of by the will. This is a convenient and efficient way for individuals to distribute small items to various beneficiaries. For your convenience we have included a link on our web site where you can download a Personal Property Disposition spreadsheet.

 Visit **WWW.DRBILLCLARK.COM** and click on *The Next Step tab*.

Having the ability to access sound judgement and not default to emotional reactions when dealing with sensitive family matters such as inheritance and finances is key. Seeking input from an unbiased professional on the outside can mean the difference between a family discussion and its total destruction. If Mary Ann had consulted with a financial advisor, they could have assisted her in dealing with Marcus' demands, and given her a better understanding of the sacrifice she was making by giving him the additional funds. It is not uncommon in such conflicts that the presence of a third party in the room can totally change the dynamics of the situation.

As in the case of James and Susan, a financial advisor could have helped them evaluate the investment of their money into their children's home, giving them a better understanding of the risk they were taking and possibly helping them to avoid that loss. In both cases you see how critical it is that you evaluate your financial condition, ensuring you have the necessary funds for your taxes, your future and emergencies first. Then if you have additional funds, you can help your children, stepchildren, grandchildren or whomever is in need.

No matter your present status - married, single, divorced or widowed - getting good quality financial counseling on what you need to do to secure your future is very important.

With emotions raw and the outlook confused, it is very important to receive counsel from someone you trust. This can be a family member or friend that has already experienced the loss or divorce. It is our hope that you have a trusted financial advisor that can walk with you through the questions and concerns that you are experiencing.

"PEOPLE FIND WAYS TO GET
THE MONEY FOR THINGS
THEY REALLY WANT."

Where Should I Live?

Phil & Clara's Story

Phil and I had a wonderful home in the country on a moderate-size ranch where we raised horses. This was a life we dearly loved for over 45 years, and when Phil passed away, I was faced with the reality of handling the ranch without him. I needed to either sell it, leaving behind a huge part of my heart and soul, or find a way to try to deal with the day-to-day work and responsibilities on my own. I am a rather stubborn woman, and since I was still very active and in good heath, I initially chose to keep the ranch and attempted to run it by myself.

As the first few weeks passed, I realized that while I could juggle the bookkeeping and general office things for the ranch, the amount of physical labor required to do what Phil had always tended to was more than I could handle. But I was not willing to sell the ranch just yet. I decided instead to hire a few part time helpers to assist me on the larger tasks, while trying to still do the majority of the smaller chores. This did help relieve some of the load, but deep down I knew that my days on my beloved ranch were drawing to an end.

Then one day while cleaning out one of the stalls, a huge gust of wind caught the barn door, slamming it into my back and head. I was thrown to the ground and was knocked unconscious for a brief time. When I did come to, I found that my legs were not able to function properly, and my cell phone was no longer in my pocket. After scooting around in the hay, I managed to locate my cell phone and call for help.

The hospital determined that I had in fact sustained some brain injury from the accident. My recovery would require a brief hospital stay and some rehab to regain the full use of my legs. That, consequently, was the end of my life on the ranch, and I reluctantly put it up for sale. The market was not the best at that time, so I was forced to ask a lower price than I wanted to get a quick sale. Parting with the ranch was a very painful decision, and going from a sprawling home to something a fraction of that size would require some serious downsizing. But I was determined to face this head on, so I began the process of auctioning off my horses and belongings.

But selling my ranch and its contents only resolved part of my dilemma - the second part was deciding where I was to live once I recovered from my injury. Phil and I had two grown children who lived on opposites sides of the country. We had always been thankful that our ranch was right in the middle of their worlds, allowing us a shorter distance to travel to see each of them while offering them each a place to meet with us. With the ranch now sold, I was forced to make a decision. No matter which one I located close to, one of their families would be many hundreds of miles away. And then on top of that decision I was looking at my options of choosing to live with my kids or opting for a retirement facility of some sort. As I thought over each of these options, I could see pros and cons to each, but there was not a clear solution. This was one of the toughest decisions I had to face after Phi's death. I realized that I needed an unbiased and informed individual to help me make this difficult choice, so I contacted my financial advisor.

From Dr. Bill

One of the most important issues you face when trying to decide where to live is cost-of-living. Cost-of-living is based on food, health care, housing, recreation, taxes, and transportation. Because your income will change after the loss of a mate, it is important to reassess your budget during this period. As in Clara's case, you can see that the decision process of where to live is not a simple one. There are multiple options and many things to consider before making this decision. This can be done individually or with the help of a financial planner.

Remaining in your present home or residence

Consider your answer to the following questions: Is your present home/ residence paid for? If not, what are your monthly payments and are you able to remain there on the income you will now be receiving? Will you be able to manage the upkeep of the lawn, garden and maintenance of this home by yourself or can you afford to pay for someone to do this for you? Is your home in an area you feel safe to remain in now that you are alone? Will your home require any major repairs in the next few years such as AC, roof or kitchen appliance replacement, just to name a few? Do you have good neighbors who could assist you if you did have an emergency? Is your home close to your network of family and/or friends?

Choosing to relocate to a smaller home/residence

Consider your answer to the following questions: What will this move cost to make? Will your new residence allow you to take the most precious things with you, or will you be forced to part with some of these belongings? If you must sell or give away some of these things, then you must choose the most necessary items to go with you and choose a place that will accommodate them. If leasing, what form of lease agreement must you sign? Is the rental property located in an area where you feel safe? Is the area well lit and does it have on-site security available? If purchasing a smaller home, evaluate all the things under the previous section with the new residence in mind. If you are selling your present home, what is the state of the housing market for your area? Will you be able to get most, if not all, of your investment from this property if it does sell? What is your back up plan if it does not sell?

Moving to a retirement facility

Note: This list of questions following each type of arrangement is not all-inclusive. These are simply basic questions that every potential resident of a retirement community should have answered.

Within this one option there are many additional choices for you to consider. These facilities/communities range from a month-to-month rental in an apartment setting, designated for independent seniors who are self sufficient all the way to fully assisted-living quarters staffed by 24-hour nursing professionals.

Independent living arrangements usually try to integrate a home-like environment and services for seniors who need very little supervision. Services will vary so be sure to inquire what is included and what might be additional costs. Typically, insurance will not cover or assist you with this choice of living arrangement. Activities vary widely based on the communities. When looking at what the facility offers, think about your preferences. Some enjoy residence-scheduled activities while other don't; inquire as to how much input residents have on the activities that are offered.

A Few Good Questions:

- What do you really need and/or want from this type of facility?
- What is the purchase or "buy-in" price tag, if there is one for this facility?

- Will this buy-in cost be in addition to your monthly expenses and leave you enough funds for your daily living expenses and needs?

- In addition, if yours is a large purchase/buy-in cost, ask them about what percentage of that deposit your family will get back once you have passed away. These funds are not at your disposal to use, but it can be part of your inheritance for your children.

- Is there a deposit and/or a waiting list that you need to be on to be able to get into this community? Is that deposit refundable?

- Do you want a one or two bedroom residence?

- Do you prefer a certain floor plan or easy access to outside doors?

- Will they allow pets?

- Do they offer smoking or non-smoking units? Do they have designated smoking areas?

- Do you need wheelchair access to your kitchen/bath and living quarters?

- Will you be responsible for your own housekeeping or will the facility maintain that for you? If so, is there an additional charge for that service?

- If you will be doing your own housekeeping, consider what you are physically able to manage. Do not choose a place that is a stretch for your present health condition, keeping in mind that your strength and stamina could decline.

- What form of laundry services will be available?

- Do you want to cook your own meals, or do you prefer to eat your meals with others in a common eating area? Or a combination of both options?

- If you choose a facility that offers a meal option, is it an additional price on a month-to-month basis or part of the overall package? What happens if you miss a meal or you are too sick to eat with them?

- Do you have a special diet? If so, will this facility accommodate that diet for you?

- If you will be cooking, how far will you have to carry your groceries from the parking lot?

- Do you have a car that you intend to take with you? If so, what are the parking options? Do you need a covered parking lot for your area of the country or is an uncovered lot sufficient?

- Will you be assigned a parking space, and, if not, what is the availability of the parking spots on a daily basis? Is the parking lot well lit? And, if needed, are there adequate handicap parking spaces?

- Is this community in a safe area of town?

- Does the facility offer any transportation assistance to doctor appointments or area stores if needed?

- Is this facility close to drug stores, grocery stores and/or medical offices?

- Does the facility offer or allow you to have access to medical assistance if you should need it?

- Is renters insurance required?

- Is this facility locked and/or monitored by a security firm? How easily can people gain access into this facility?

- Under what conditions will the community terminate the lease agreement?

- How long has this community been established?

- What maintenance service will the facility provide for your residence and how quickly do they respond?

Assisted living, whether temporary or long term, provides assistance 24 hours a day. This usually includes meals, assistance with bathing/ dressing/ medications and more. Some also offer 24-hour nursing supervision if needed. Insurance may cover a portion of these expenses, but not all facilities accept Medicaid, Medicare or your individual insurance. Discuss with the Admissions Director the specifics of your situation to determine what they accept and if you will be able to get financial assistance. If you feel that your health is deteriorating to the point that this option is necessary, you are looking at a monthly price tag from $4,000 to $7,000 based on the level of care needed. A financial advisor would be the best person to help you assess your financial situation and your level of need to determine what you can afford.

A Few Good Questions:

- What is the resident to staff ratio?

- What is the criteria for admission?

- If you require specific medical attention, it is also necessary to evaluate the ability of a facility to provide the level and quality of medical care needed.

- Determine the baseline fee and what that price will provide in the way of services. What are the additional charges for other services/ products?

- What initial payment or deposit is required, and is any of it refundable?

- Is there a waiting list?

- What happens to your room if you were to be hospitalized for an extended period of time, and what will you be required to continue to pay for?

- What happens to you if your funds run out?
- Do they require renter's insurance?
- Is this facility safe and secure? Do they enforce a lock down of exterior doors, and if so when?
- How does a resident call for help, and how quickly will someone respond?
- What is the grievance procedure for this facility should you not be satisfied with the service or quality of care?

It is important to match your ability with the extent of choices and opportunities offered by the facility, as well as the limitations it will impose upon you. Consider those facilities which earn superior ratings on their annual state/joint commission surveys. All facilities are required to post their survey results. Be sure to tour several facilities and take into consideration cleanliness and amount of nursing supervision you see while there. Take the time to talk with staff and residents about the quality of care in that facility. And over all, trust your instincts.

Moving in with Family Members

A few things to consider: Is this home suitable for your present level of health? Does this home require you to use stairs regularly? If so, is that an issue? Do they have pets and, if so, is that a potential problem for you? Will you have a space/room that is totally separate from the rest of the family providing you some privacy? Does this family have children, and, if so, will their activity level be a problem for you to deal with on a daily basis? Will the family expect you to baby-sit regularly for them? How welcome do you feel in their home when you have gone for short stays? Do you have a good relationship with the family members? Cohabitation with loved ones is harder than brief visits, so if this option ends up not working, what is your back up plan? Do they live in an area of town that is familiar to you or will you be adjusting to a whole new circle of stores, churches, friends and hospitals? Will they want you to pay a monthly amount to live with them? Is the climate or region in which they live suitable for your health? How willing are they to assist you should you should need it?

 ## Veteran Benefits for Long-Term Care

Seniors who are veterans or the spouse of a veteran are often unaware of a little-known veterans benefit called "aid-and-attendance" that helps pay for long-term care for those who have difficulty with bathing, dressing and/or fixing meals. This benefit eases a big financial burden for disabled older adults.

Seniors who can no longer care for themselves are forced to consider moving into assisted-living communities or hiring in-home caregivers; the cost of these choices can be staggering. Neither Medicare nor Medicaid typically assist with these options, and if you do not have long-term insurance, the expense can wipe out your retirement in a few short years. For those qualifying for this assistance, it can add up to significant help toward the financial burden.

The Aid-and-Attendance pension benefit requires extensive documentation. Along with military discharge papers and a physician's written evaluation, there are pages of questions you must thoroughly answer and a financial assessment must be submitted. Then once you have mailed the package it can take up to 4-6 months for the Department of Veterans Affairs to process it, assuming all the documentation is correct. One blessing is that once the benefit is approved, it is retroactive to when the senior applied. You will find that the process is well worth the effort because the payment of $1,000 to nearly $2,000 a month will go a long way toward providing you or your loved one the necessary care. To learn if you are eligible for this assistance and to get the list of necessary documentation call the VA at 1-800-827-1000 or visit **WWW.VA.GOV** today. Veterans or next-of-kin may access military discharge documents at **WWW.VETRECS.ARCHIVES.GOV**.

"DO YOU TAKE COUPONS?"

Whom Do I Trust?

Emma & Warren's Story

When Warren was diagnosed with cancer, it motivated us to find some trustworthy professionals to help us get our financial documents in order. Warren was especially cautious about turning over our sensitive information to people we barely knew. How could we trust that they would be honest? We would be making some long term decisions based on their advice which would directly affect my future when Warren was gone. It was not easy, but we did manage to find a great team.

Warren's engineering mind was very detailed and organized. He had managed all of our accounting and financial issues throughout our entire marriage. I am what you might call the creative one, and, consequently, I don't have a detailed bone in my body. Because of that, Warren knew that he needed to get someone to oversee these things for me. But finding the right match for us was a bit of a challenge. We had been fortunate to have a great CPA who had been doing our taxes for a number of years, so we started with him. He met us and looked over our taxes and told us that things were in good order as we faced Warren's dark future. He assured me that I could simply bring him my taxes next year and he would take care of everything for me.

One down with several more professionals to locate. As we began our search for a financial advisor, we quickly realized that not all of these professionals had our best interests in mind. Some were more concerned with lining their own pockets with our money. One even told us we did not have a large enough portfolio for him to assist us. A few would not call us back, so that helped us to decide that they would not be a good match. Consequently, we walked out of several financial offices before finding one that was a fit. He was very qualified, had great references, was relational and easy to communicate with and was willing to help us get our financial investments in order. The Financial Investment Advisor did not rush our consultation session, but he took detailed notes and asked many open-ended questions about what we needed from him.

We wanted to know if our present investments were suitable for our future or if we needed to change them in any way. He assured us that our investments were on track with what we needed, so we did not have to change anything. He then developed a comprehensive financial strategy that he later explained to us in detail. He even submitted his numbers and calculations to Warren for examination, knowing how detail-oriented he was. That really impressed Warren and went a long way to helping us feel confident that he was honest and we had chosen wisely. In addition, we were relieved to see that with his plan I would be provided for with a significant income and even some financial reserves for emergencies. He assured me that he would be easily accessible, should I need anything else.

Next on our list was finding a good attorney. Our financial advisor gave us a short list of attorneys to start with, so we set up meetings with them. We were able to quickly find one that we both were comfortable with, and he came with a list of very satisfied clients. He took care of updating our wills, getting a Power of Attorney written as well as a living will, in addition to setting up a revocable living trust so when Warren did meet the Lord, there would be a seamless passing of our assets to me. That was a new term to me, but it sure was one of the best things we did.

We spent weeks going in and out of multiple advisors' offices - I was very thankful to have Warren by my side to make these various decisions. And I cannot tell you how much peace it gave me just knowing that I had this awesome team of professionals to call on if I had any questions.

From Dr. Bill

After over 30 years in practice, I have discovered that many times financial advisors have their own agenda, desiring to make large commissions by managing assets. It is critical that a well-thought-out financial plan and strategy be established with conservative, well-defined goals in order to meet the income objectives as well as the accumulation objectives for the client. If you discover that your financial advisor or stock broker seems to be pushing investments versus strategies on you, then it's probably a good idea to be shopping around for a new Registered Investment Advisor.

A good financial professional or advisor can help you overcome obstacles and achieve your dreams. If you aren't currently working with one, or find you need a new one, these tips may help you find one that's right for you. Usually an independent person, such as a financial planner, has the widow's best interest at heart instead of his or her pocketbook in making a commission or fee.

Decide what your goal is before seeking a financial advisor. What services are you looking for? Are you looking for someone to just manage your investment portfolio? Or are you looking for someone to do more financial planning, including life insurance, taxes and retirement planning? Do you have any estate planning or healthcare needs? These items are important because you want someone who has experience with your specific needs. Some advisors just manage your investment account, while others provide additional services for clients.

Experience is important. In general the longer someone has been in the business, the more insights they might have on what works and what doesn't. While you don't have to only seek individuals with gray hair, you do not want to risk your future with an inexperienced professional. On the other hand, someone with less experience but more recent education and training may be more open to new products and strategies. Regardless, look for someone with a record of success and a list of highly satisfied clients. Personal referrals are very helpful, but you can also check a professional's reputation further by contacting the Securities and Exchange Commission or the state regulatory agencies for complaints.

There are a number of credentials that financial advisors often have. Ask for an explanation of these credentials. They represent expertise in certain areas of the financial industry. Knowing what they mean will help you decide which type of expertise you want in an advisor.

- **RIA** - Registered Investment Advisor
- **CLU** - One who is skilled in most insurance contracts and estate planning
- **ChFC** - One who is skilled in total financial planning, investments, tax, estate, cash management, insurance
- **CFP** - One who is skilled in total financial planning, investments, tax, estate, cash management, insurance
- **CFA** - One who is skilled in evaluating financial statements for businesses
- **CPA** - One who is skilled in advising and preparation of both simple and complicated income and estate tax returns

Ask what licenses they hold and if they are registered with the SEC, a state, or the Financial Industry Regulatory Authority (FINRA).

Be sure to meet potential advisors "face to face" to make sure they are a good match for you personally. Ability to communicate with your advisor is also very important. Find out how often the advisor speaks to their clients. Is it on a regular basis, or do they just respond to questions and/or phone calls? And ask what a normal response time is from them when you do have a question. Inquire about regular reports on your portfolio activity as well as how often they will review your portfolio with you.

Ask the financial planner about the type of clients and financial situations he typically likes to work with. Some planners prefer to develop one plan by bringing together all of your financial goals. Others provide advice on specific areas, as needed. Make sure the planner's viewpoint on investing is not too cautious or overly aggressive for you. Some planners require you to have a certain net worth before offering services. Find out if the planner will carry out the financial recommendations developed for you or if you must go elsewhere. Some areas to inquire about their experience are retirement planning, investment planning, tax planning, estate planning, insurance planning and integrated planning just to name a few.

The financial planner may work with you himself or have others in the office assist him or her. You may want to meet everyone who will be working with you. If the planner works with professionals outside his own practice (such as attorneys, insurance agents or tax specialists) to develop or carry out financial planning recommendations, get a list of their names to check on their backgrounds.

Next discuss with the advisor what his fees will be for his services and who directly pays that fee. Financial planners can be paid in several ways:

- A salary paid by the company for which they work
- Fees based on an hourly rate, a flat rate or on a percentage of your assets and /or income
- Commission paid by a third party from the products sold to you to carry out the financial planning recommendations
- Combination of fees and commissions

While the amount you pay the planner will depend on your particular needs, the financial planner should be able to provide you with an estimate of possible costs based on the work to be performed. Such costs would include the planner's hourly rates or flat fees or the percentage he would receive as commission on money being managed.

And finally, ask the planner to provide you with a written agreement that details the services that will be provided. Keep this document in your files for future reference.

"MY HEART CANDY SAYS,
'FOR ALL YOUR BUSINESS NEEDS CONTACT
CLARK FINANCIAL GROUP.'"

When a Marriage Ends

Jack & Beverly's Story

I had heard it stated that when a marriage disintegrates, it is almost like a death in the family. After going through this personally, I would agree with that statement. Jack and I were married for five years. The first three were good years, or so I thought. Our lives were filled with love and dreams of a future we would share together. Jack, being the more detailed one, offered to take care of all of our finances. He paid our bills, managed our bank accounts and attended to our insurance. I never saw the need to ask about what he spent or how our finances were being used. I assumed that he was managing our finances wisely and making good financial decisions for our future. That was, as it turned out, a big mistake.

One day I came home from work to find that every trace of our life together was gone. He had taken his clothes and personal belongings, and his car was missing. Jack had simply walked away from our marriage, taking all that he valued with him. I was completely shocked; there had been no indication of his unhappiness with me or our marriage prior to that moment. Sadly, on that day, everything I had believed about him and our marriage was shattered into pieces.

It was not long after he left that I realized I knew next to nothing about our present financial situation, other than where our bank was located. I had to stop my emotional spiral long enough to find out what else he had taken. I grabbed my car keys and drove to the bank to see what funds were left in our checking and savings accounts. When I inquired about them, I was informed that both were totally empty. He had taken all our money and left me with absolutely nothing. I felt incredibly disillusioned and naïve. How could I have been so wrong about this man I had loved?

That week, as bills began arriving in the mail, I realized for the first time that all our combined debt was totally in my name. He had managed to accumulate a sizeable amount in just a few short years. The charges he had racked up were staggering. How could I have been so blind?

There was no time to feel sorry for myself. I had to find a way to fix the mess I now found myself in. First, I opened my own bank account and directed my paychecks to this new account, insuring he would not have access to them. I could not do anything about the funds he had taken, but I sure could keep him from getting any more. Then I had to figure out what I was now legally responsible for in the way of the debt. I needed to get in touch with each of the creditors so that I could arrange payment and remove Jack's name off all the accounts. And I needed to contact a good lawyer - I needed sound advice on what to do next.

I also realized that I needed to have a crash course on finances, so with the help of a wise financial advisor, I began to undo the damage that he had done to my fiances and my credit score. In the future, if I do remarry, I will be more informed and have an active part of each financial decision, I will not let myself get caught in that trap again.

From Dr. Bill

Again, this story illustrates the importance of knowing your financial circumstances and having all the details of your financial information on hand. It is every person's responsibility to know their situation and have the important details on file. If you don't know any part of your own financial situation, it's up to you to look into it immediately.

You can use the same spreadsheet from chapter one to list your important account information. The list of questions from chapter one is also good for this same circumstance. Young married couples should work together toward their financial future. The days of one working to bring in the money and the other overseeing their finances are over. It's only smart for the couple to work as a team in their marriage and their finances.

As you can see from Beverly's experience, the sudden exit of your spouse can cause severe emotional and financial trauma. DO NOT go it alone. Get help from those who can best help you. Don't wait. Time is of the essence. Make the call. You will be very glad you did.

All too often we counsel clients on how to work out of a disaster like the one described above. Here are the steps you need to do to protect yourself:

1. Hire a good attorney that specializes in debt resolution.

2. Change financial institutions NOW and have your income, (social security, annuity payments, pension, etc) changed to the new account.

3. Contact the creditors and communicate what has been discovered. Take good notes of what was said, to whom you spoke, date and time.

4. Set up a reasonable budget (see page 49) and stick to it.

5. Establish an emergency fund. This is an amount of money equal to 3-6 months of your living expenses.

6. Hire a financial advisor, not a financial sales person.

7. Did I mention, you need to hire a GOOD attorney who SPECIALIZES in debt resolution!

"THIS IS AN END-OF-YEAR
CLEARANCE SALE,
NOT A 'CLARENCE' SALE."

Gathering, Filing & Storing Important Documents & Information

Safety Deposit Box

A safety deposit box serves several functions - namely keeping your important documents or other items in a secure, off-site location. In many cases, a safety deposit box is probably safer than a lock box in your home, it is more difficult to break into and limits access. But that limited access can also be a problem if you need quick access to certain documents or other valuables.

For that reason, DO NOT keep documents or other valuables you may need at a moment's notice in a safety deposit box, including your passport, **original** copies of your will, estate plans, power of attorney, burial preference, medical documents, living will, and similar items. In the event of your death it may take a court order to unseal your safety deposit box, causing a delay in settling your estate. In addition, it is wise to leave copies of your will with your estate executor and your attorney.

A safety deposit box can be rented at a local bank or credit union for a relatively low cost, starting around $20 for a small box. Be sure to check as prices and policies can vary greatly from one location to another. Asking a lawyer, accountant, friend or relative to co-sign the safety deposit box account with you is another option. Always keep the key in a safe location (fireproof safe) and it is wise to give a duplicate key to a trusted individual.

Fireproof Safe

Another option is a secure fireproof safe that you keep at home. In many cases this is sufficient, but you will need to take into account your own personal situation and how valuable your important documents or other items are that you intend to store. When investing in a fireproof safe, buy one that is large enough to store your important documents but small enough to move by yourself if you have to evacuate your home. Unfortunately, even a fireproof safe can melt in a very hot fire. However, a safe will withstand fire much better than a shoebox or cardboard box! Check into the Fire Ratings for the models you are considering. The UL (Underwriter's Laboratories) rating will list a number representing the allowed internal temperature of that item when exposed to 1700 degrees for one hour. Recommended document storage is 350, while data storage (photos, CD, DVD, Flash Drives and other electronic media suffer damage at a temp of 140) should be stored in a UL rating of 125 or lower.

Organizing your Documents

A good record keeping system will allow someone who is unfamiliar with the system to locate important documents, maintain records and prepare reports in case of an emergency. Your filing system doesn't have to be elaborate, but it should be organized. Office supply stores have a variety of folders and envelopes available that help separate papers into categories. Colored folders can be helpful, in addition to expandable file folders that hold all your papers in one place. Putting irreplaceable items into waterproof water tight bags before placing them into your fireproof safe is an additional protection for your documents. Creating a quick reference binder (listing all your documents & location) will help you manage your financial affairs.

Where to Start:

Gather your important papers from throughout the house. Divide your file folders into three major areas:

- Current records
- Inactive records
- Permanent records

Current files should include employment records, credit card information, insurance policies, family health records, warranties and guarantees, education records, bank statements, a household inventory, tax records and canceled checks. These headings may be used as a basis for your filing system.

Inactive files are used to store the items from the current files that are three years old. Go through the current files once a year. Discard unneeded items and transfer others to inactive storage. A good time to make transfers is the first of the year when you work on your income tax forms. File headings would be the same as for current files.

Permanent records are very important papers, ones that should be kept safe in a safe deposit box or fireproof (and waterproof) storage container indefinitely.

By maintaining a comprehensive record of your personal affairs, you can keep important information available for easy access. In times of emergency, it is important that you and your family be able to take immediate action with regard to financial affairs. Also, an inventory is invaluable when death occurs. The following pages will assist you in keeping accurate records. I strongly encourage a once-a-year update of this information.

HOME FIREPROOF DOCUMENT INFO:

NOTE - ORIGINAL DOCUMENTS ARE STORED HERE

Birth/Death Certificates	Copies of drivers licenses
Adoption Certificates	Copies of other items in your wallet
Will /Living Wills	List of credit card account numbers
Marriage Certificate	Divorce/Separation Decrees
Social Security Cards	Custody agreements
Real Estate Deeds	Passports
Vehicle titles/lease	Military Records
Other real estate papers	Citizenship naturalization papers

Inventory of household items

Power of Attorney (durable and medical)

Personal Property Memorandum

Records of jointly owned property

Paid Mortgage or Loan Contracts

Insurance policies, contact info and details

Warranties & Instruction Manuals/Books

Investment & Banking Information

Copyrights and patents

Key to Safety Deposit Box - inventory of safety deposit box

PERSONAL INFORMATION

Cemetery deeds-burial instructions

Diplomas - education records

Investment Information

Medical Records-phone numbers, physicians, allergies, operations, Medicare & Medicaid information, list of prescription medications, blood type

CD/DVD/Jump drives with important files from your computer

Critical Personal Information - SEE PAGES 96-102 FOR EXAMPLES

Credit card, debt, atm, smart accounts/details

Debt information

Computer password master list

Information you can keep in a safety deposit box -
or other secure location.

SAFETY DEPOSIT DOCUMENTS:

COPIES ONLY -KEEP ORIGINALS IN A FIREPROOF SAFE AT HOME

Copies of Birth/Death Certificates
Copies of Adoption Certificates
Copies of Will /Living Wills
Copies of Marriage Certificate
Copies of Social Security Cards
Real Estate Deeds
Copies of vehicle titles/lease
Copies of drivers licenses
Copies of other items in your wallet
List of credit card account numbers
Copies of Divorce/ Separation Decrees
Copies of Custody agreements
Inventory of household items
Other real estate papers
Jewelry, coins, collectibles or other hard to replace items
Copies of Military Records
Citizenship naturalization papers
Copies of Power of Attorney (durable and medical)
Paid Mortgage or Loan Contracts
Personal Property Memorandum
Records of jointly owned property
Insurance policies

Make a detailed list of everything you are leaving in the safety deposit box and keep that in your fireproof box or other secure location at home. This will insure that when needed documents can be easily located.

Important Personal Information:

This information should be completed and updated on a yearly basis to insure information is current. The following form will help you organize and record valuable data. Once completed, this information should be secured and accessible only by authorized individuals. It is NOT intended in any way to serve as a legal document.

PERSONAL DIRECTORY INFO
FILL OUT FOR HUSBAND & WIFE SEPARATELY
Today's Date:
Name:
Address:
City: ST: Zip:
Home Telephone: # of yrs at present address:
Prior Address:
Social Security #:
Date of Birth: Citizen of:
Place of Birth:
Marital Status: ☐ Married ☐ Divorced ☐ Widower ☐ Single
Full Name of Father:
Father's Place of Birth:
Father's Date of Birth:
Father's Date of Death: His Age at Death:
Full Name of Mother (MAIDEN NAME):
Mother's Place of Birth:
Mother's Date of Birth:
Mother's Date of Death: Her Age at Death:

PERSONAL DIRECTORY INFO CONTINUED
FILL OUT FOR HUSBAND & WIFE SEPARATELY

SCHOOLS ATTENDED:

School Name:

From: To: Highest Grade or Degree:

School Name:

From: To: Highest Grade or Degree:

School Name:

From: To: Highest Grade or Degree:

FRATERNITIES OR HONOR SOCIETIES:

Group Name:

From: To: Position Held:

Group Name:

From: To: Position Held:

CIVIC OR PUBLIC OFFICES HELD:

Office Name:

From: To: Where:

Office Name:

From: To: Where:

SPECIAL ACHIEVEMENTS OR RECOGNITIONS:

ORGANIZATIONS AFFILIATIONS: (MASON, LION'S CLUB, ELK ETC)

Group Name:

Benefits Due: ☐ Yes ☐ No

PERSONAL DIRECTORY INFO CONTINUED
FILL OUT FOR HUSBAND & WIFE SEPARATELY

JOB STATISTICS:

Company:

From: To: Job Title:

Company:

From: To: Job Title:

Company:

From: To: Job Title:

Company:

From: To: Job Title:

PROFESSIONAL ACHIEVEMENTS:

MILITARY SERVICE:

Branch of Service:

Service #:

Dates of Service From: To:

Discharge Date:

Theater(s) of Service:

Grade, Rank, Rating:

Citations, Recognitions, Awards:

Discharge Papers Located at:

G.I. Insurance Policy #:

VA Claim #:

PERSONAL DIRECTORY INFO CONTINUED

FILL OUT FOR HUSBAND & WIFE SEPARATELY

RECORD OF CHILDREN:

#1 Child-Given Name:

Address:

Date of Birth: Place of Birth:

#2 Child-Given Name:

Address:

Date of Birth: Place of Birth:

#3 Child-Given Name:

Address:

Date of Birth: Place of Birth:

#4 Child-Given Name:

Address:

Date of Birth: Place of Birth:

#5 Child-Given Name:

Address:

Date of Birth: Place of Birth:

#6 Child-Given Name:

Address:

Date of Birth: Place of Birth:

#7 Child-Given Name:

Address:

Date of Birth: Place of Birth:

PERSONAL DIRECTORY INFO CONTINUED
FILL OUT FOR HUSBAND & WIFE SEPARATELY

RECORD OF SIBLINGS STILL LIVING:

#1 Sibling-Given Name:

Address:

Date of Birth: Place of Birth:

#2 Sibling-Given Name:

Address:

Date of Birth: Place of Birth:

#3 Sibling-Given Name:

Address:

Date of Birth: Place of Birth:

#4 Sibling-Given Name:

Address:

Date of Birth: Place of Birth:

#5 Sibling-Given Name:

Address:

Date of Birth: Place of Birth:

#6 Sibling-Given Name:

Address:

Date of Birth: Place of Birth:

#7 Sibling-Given Name:

Address:

Date of Birth: Place of Birth:

PERSONAL DIRECTORY INFO CONTINUED
FILL OUT FOR HUSBAND & WIFE SEPARATELY

RECORD OF DECEASED MEMBERS OF FAMILY:

#1 Name:

Relationship: Age at Death:

Cemetery: Date of Passing:

#2 Name:

Relationship: Age at Death:

Cemetery: Date of Passing:

#3 Name:

Relationship: Age at Death:

Cemetery: Date of Passing:

#4 Name:

Relationship: Age at Death:

Cemetery: Date of Passing:

#5 Name:

Relationship: Age at Death:

Cemetery: Date of Passing:

#6 Name:

Relationship: Age at Death:

Cemetery: Date of Passing:

#7 Name:

Relationship: Age at Death:

Cemetery: Date of Passing:

PERSONAL DIRECTORY INFO CONTINUED
FILL OUT FOR HUSBAND & WIFE SEPARATELY

OTHER IMPORTANT RELATIVES/SPOUSES/FRIENDS:

#1 Name:

Relationship:

If X-Spouse - Date of Marriage: Date of Divorce:

Contact Number:

Address:

#2 Name:

Relationship:

If X-Spouse - Date of Marriage: Date of Divorce:

Contact Number:

Address:

#3 Name:

Relationship:

If X-Spouse - Date of Marriage: Date of Divorce:

Contact Number:

Address:

#4 Name:

Relationship:

If X-Spouse - Date of Marriage: Date of Divorce:

Contact Number:

Address:

Bill Clark grew up in Tyler, Texas. He attended Tyler Jr. College and Oklahoma Baptist University on a trumpet and voice scholarship. After graduation, he attended Southwestern Baptist Theological Seminary in Ft. Worth and graduated with a Masters in Religious Education (Counseling). Today, Bill and his wife, Lynn, live in Frisco, Texas, a Suburb of Dallas. They have two children and seven grandchildren. Faith and family are the foundations of Bill's financial planning practice.

Bill entered the estate planning and financial services industry in 1980. Working diligently, he completed the basic and advanced certifications in financial consulting. These are the Chartered Life Underwriter and Chartered Financial Consultant. Both are from the American College in Bryn Mawr, Pennsylvania. At the same time, Bill completed his doctoral work in psychology and counseling at Cornerstone University. That was 26 years ago, and now Bill heads his own financial planning firm, Clark Financial Group, Inc., based in Frisco with offices in Richardson, Arlington, Grapevine and Fort Worth, Texas.

As a financial advisor, Bill advises people on retirement planning, estate planning, tax planning, money management, and insurance needs. His passion is helping pre-retirees and retired folks preserve and protect the assets they've worked so hard to accumulate. Bill helps his clients avoid paying unnecessary income tax, tax on social security and estate taxes. Helping clients increase their spendable income while preserving their assets is another important part of his practice. Finally, he works with his senior clients to help them avoid Medicaid spend-down of their hard earned assets when they need to turn to a nursing home for care.

Bill and his team work to develop long-term and committed relationships with their clients. "Safety of principal and preservation of the estate are the goals we work to attain for our clients." – Dr. Bill Clark

Clark Financial Group, Inc. - 6898 Lebanon Rd, Suite 101 - Frisco, TX 75034
Phone: 469-287-5657 or 888-647-1936 - Email: bill@wrclark.com
Web: www.drbillclark.com